Mandalas
A Coloring Book
Volume 2

Walter Wm. Hofheinz

Please visit ninetydays.com for more information, or contact us at the address below. Bulk purchases may also be arranged.

ISBN-13: 978-1523956876
ISBN-10: 1523956879

ninetydays press
P.O. Box 180177
Dallas, Texas 75218-0177
214.363.2400
wwh@ninetydays.com

Graphic Design and Production by
Kim Schlossberg Designs
Dallas, Texas
kimmarla.com
kim@kimmarla.com

Acknowledgments

Thanks to Kim Schlossberg, my "significant other," of Kim Schlossberg Designs, without whom this book would have been much more unlikely and difficult. Thanks also to the members of First Unitarian Church of Dallas, who view my drawing in church as an unobjectionable eccentricity.

Why Mandalas?

Almost by accident, I was introduced to the fact that an older family friend, unbeknownst to me, had for many years been drawing mandalas with pen and paper. He had received introduction to the process from a former professor, and, over the years had filled the bleak time of most faculty and committee meetings with drawing. These he gave to whoever at the meeting wanted them.

Greatly attracted, I began to draw mandalas as well, and have continued doing so for over 20 years. The most amazing thing about the process is that all are unique, although some themes repeat. For the most part, I draw in archival permanent ink, of various widths. Some I color, which is an interesting exercise, wholly apart from the original drawing, primarily using Prismacolor colored pencils. No special tools are necessary, however. My friend uses markers on copy paper much of the time. Use what is at hand!

Each of the mandalas in this book were drawn without mechanical aids of any kind, freehand, starting only with a dot in the center and eight dots at the cardinal points.

I encourage you to give the process a try. Each creator soon develops their own individual interaction with the process. Don't worry about how it will turn out; the only rule is that there are no mistakes, only unknown and unforeseen parts of the developing pattern. For a video demonstration of Walter drawing a mandala, go to ninetydays.com/video.

Enjoy!

Share what you color!

Post your colored mandalas to
Walter's Facebook page at
www.facebook.com/WalterHofheinzArt/

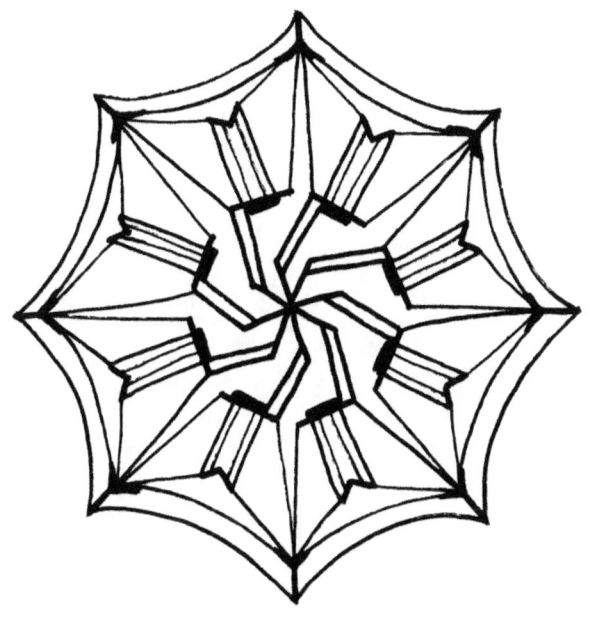

Figure 1

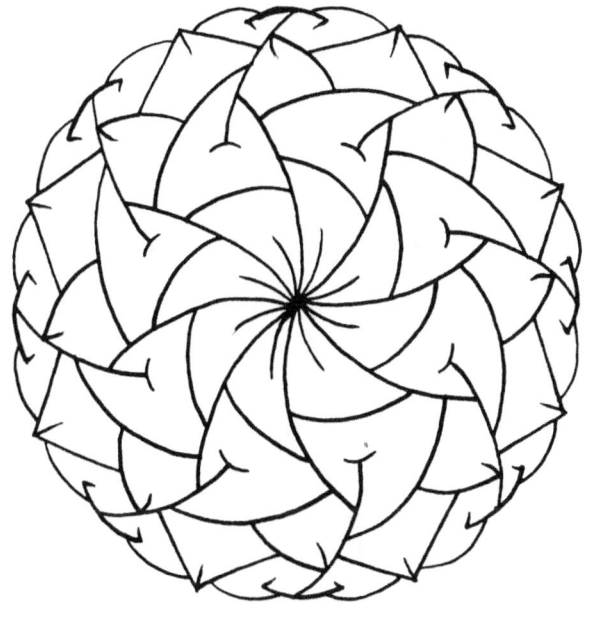

Don't let others lead you, they may be blind.
Rumi

Grace does not come easy.
quoted from "a River Runs Through It"

Figure 2

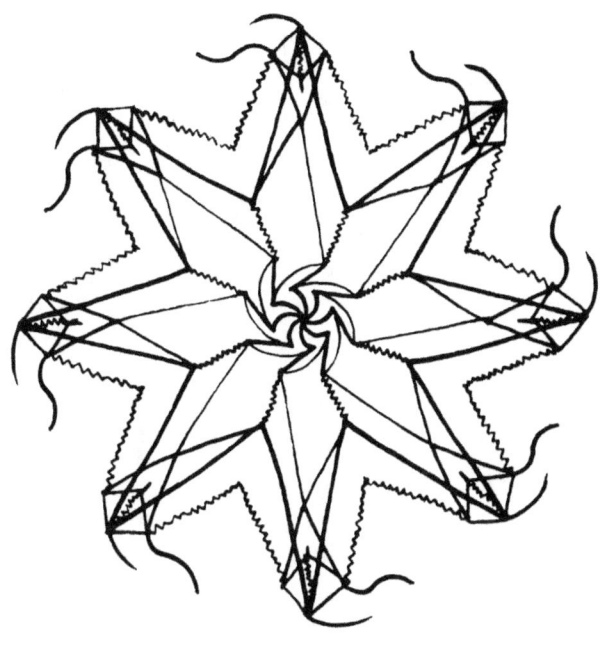

Figure 3

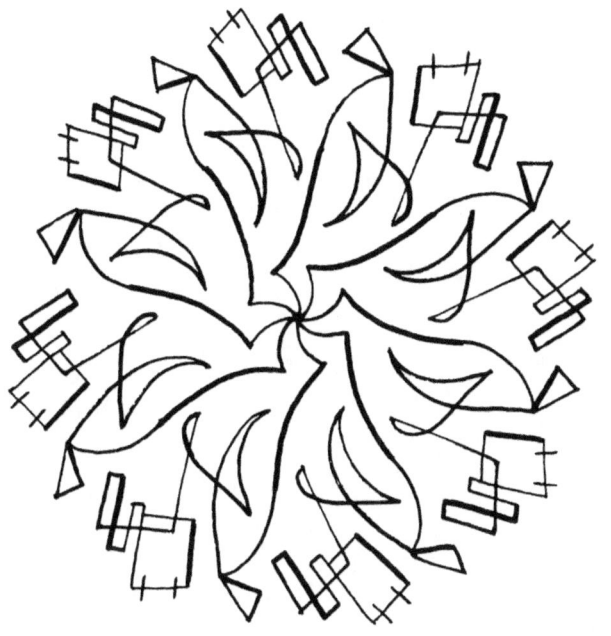

Figure 4

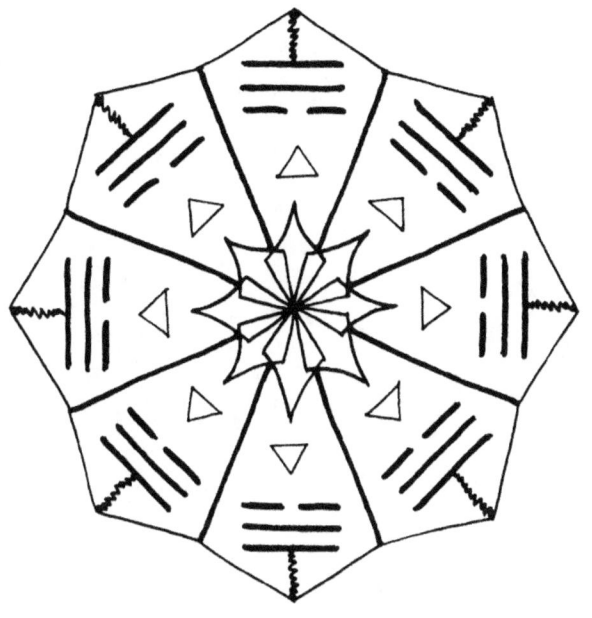

Figure 5

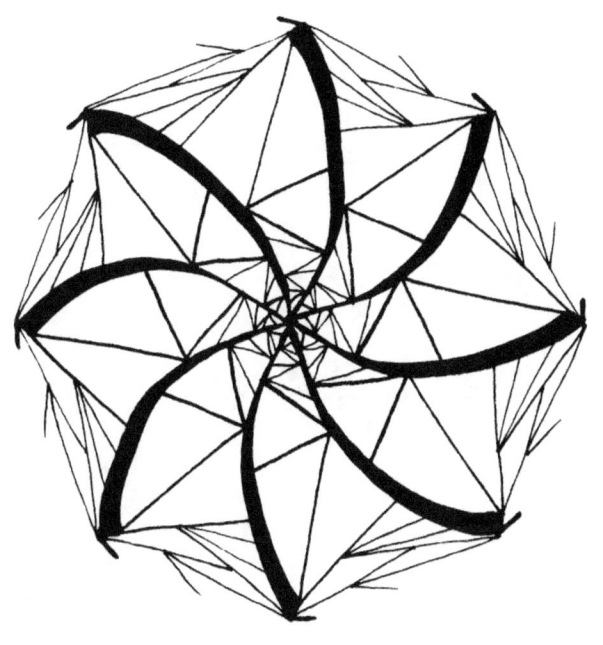

The hidden companion to our quest…
Madeleine Albright

Figure 6

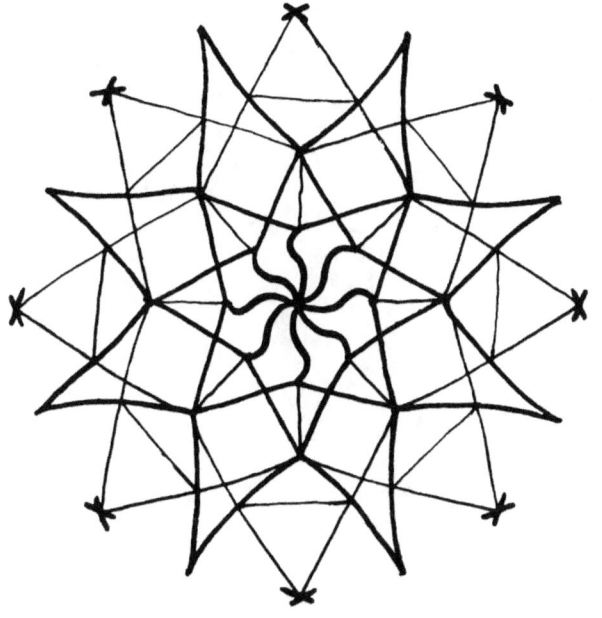

Figure 7

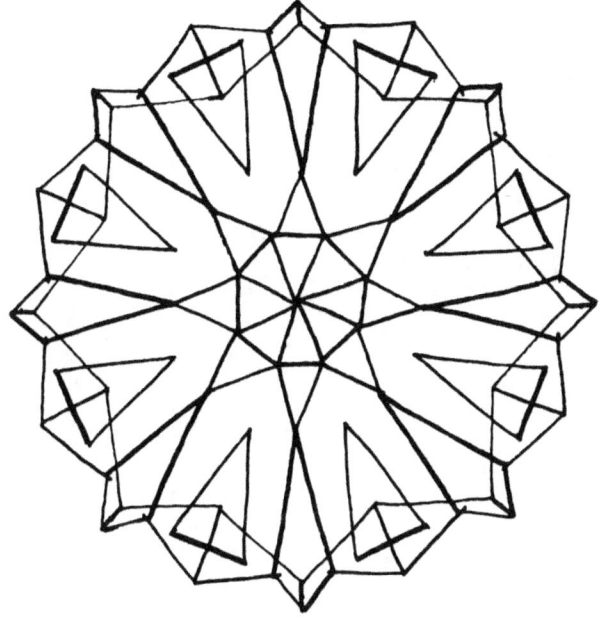

Figure 8

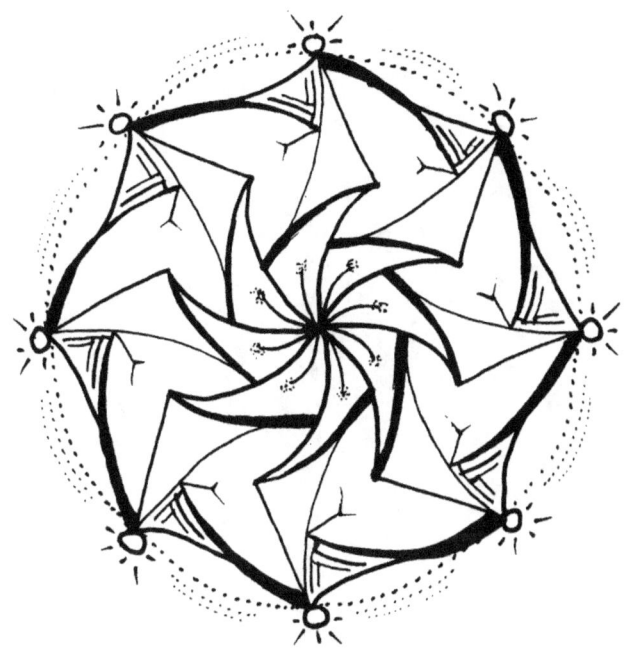

Remember what was; be inspired by what might be.

R Douglas Kohn

Figure 9

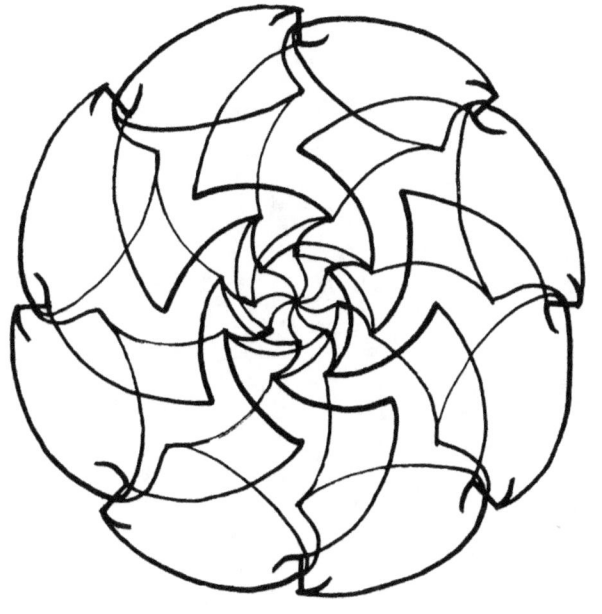

Figure 10

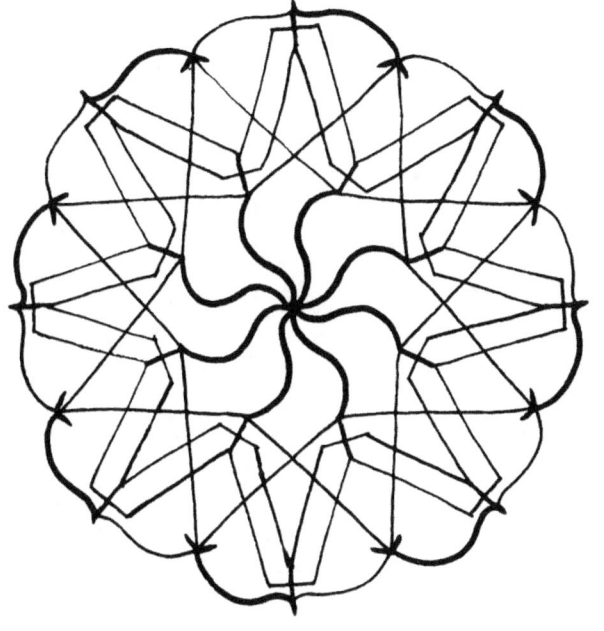

Figure 11

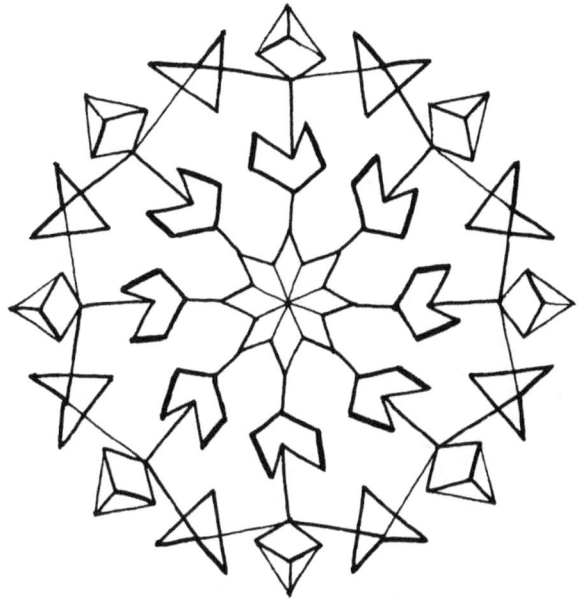

Figure 12

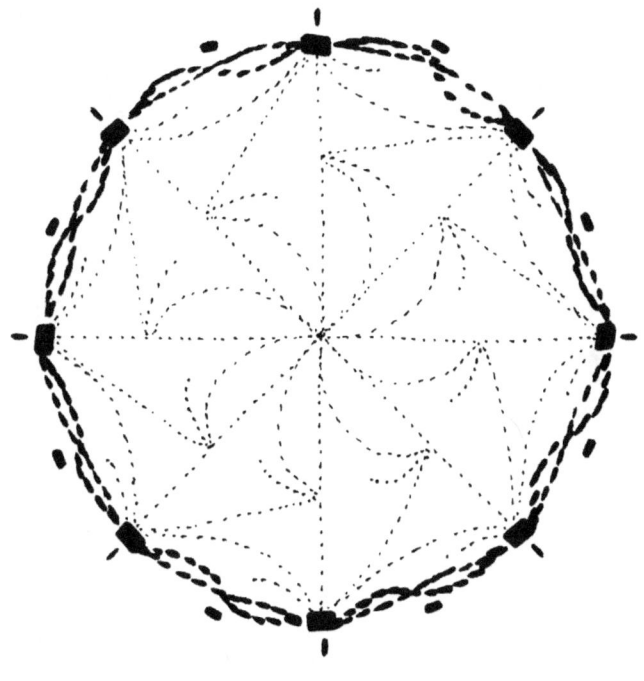

To whom do we belong? What is worthy of our devotion?

Daniel Kanter

Figure 13

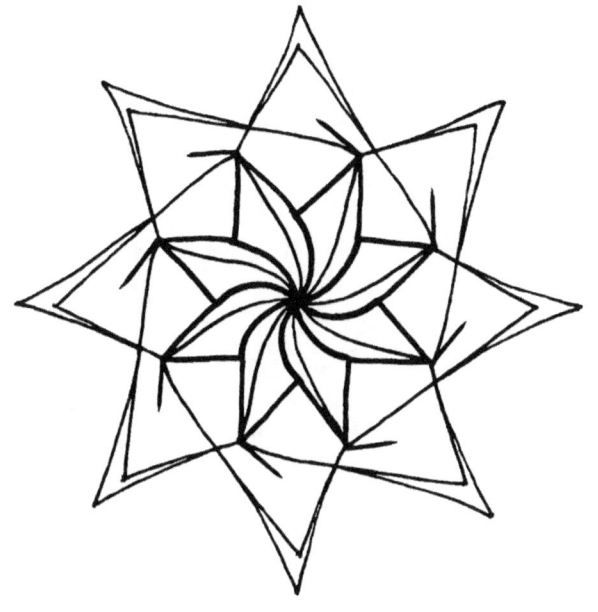

Figure 14

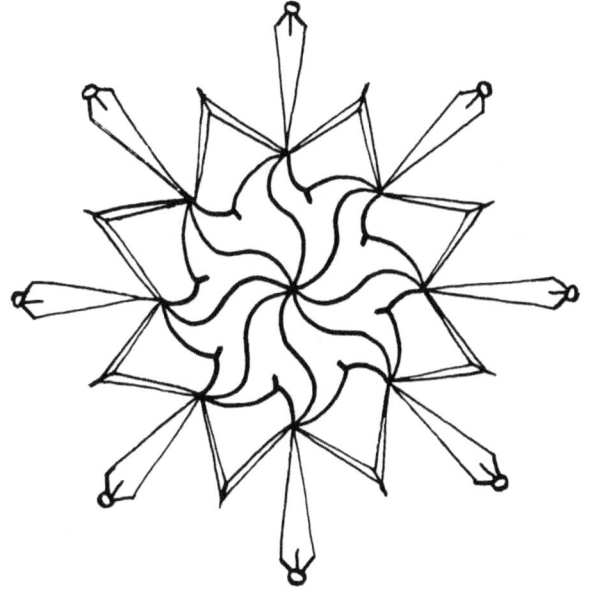

Figure 15

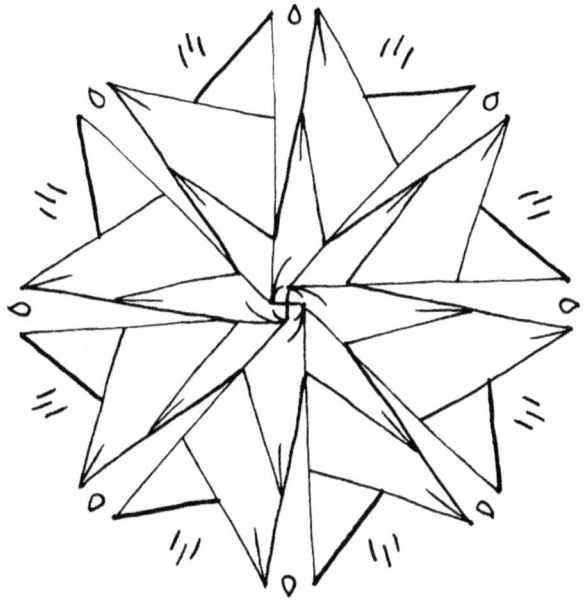

Tiptoe past the dogs of the apocalypse...
"How to Be Hopeful" *Barbara Kingsolver*

Figure 16

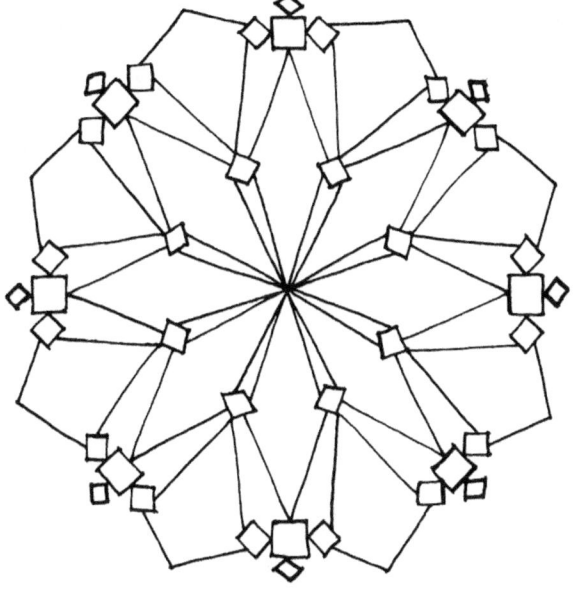

Figure 17

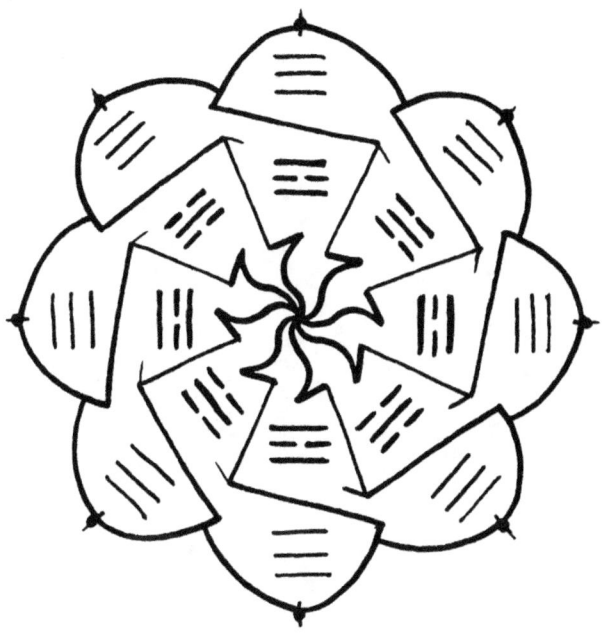

Figure 18

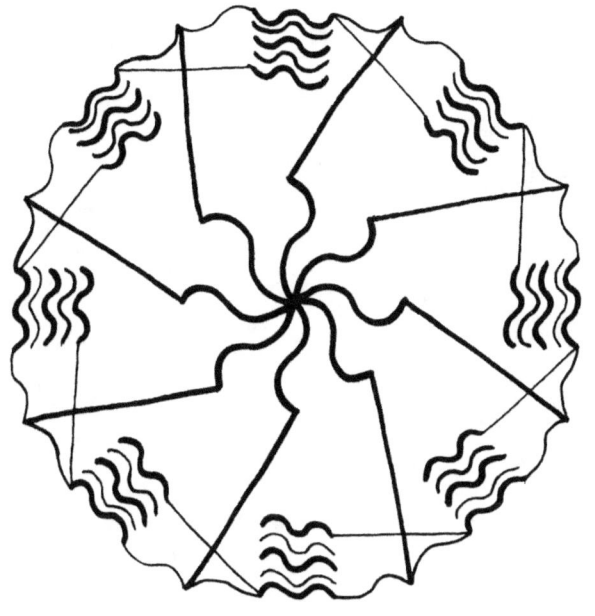

Figure 19

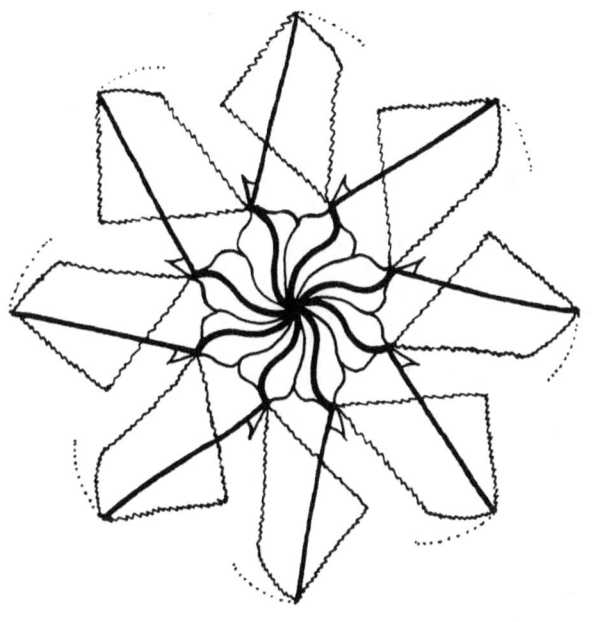

Figure 20

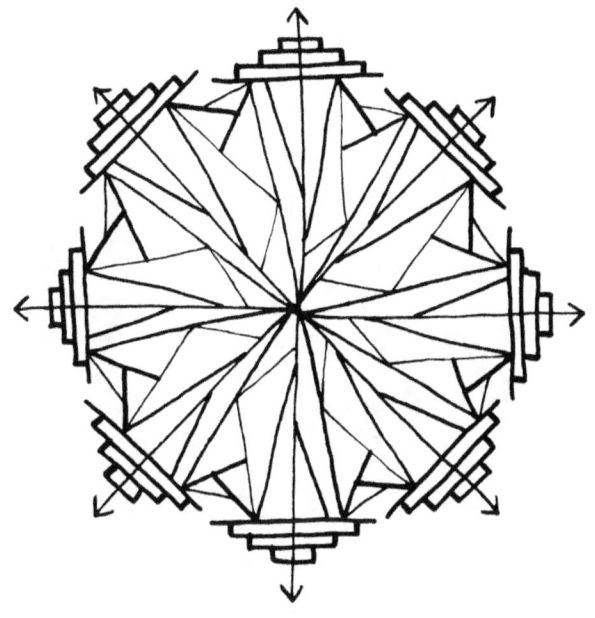

From an unwanted event came an invitation to freedom.

"The Vase," *David S. Blanchard*

Figure 21

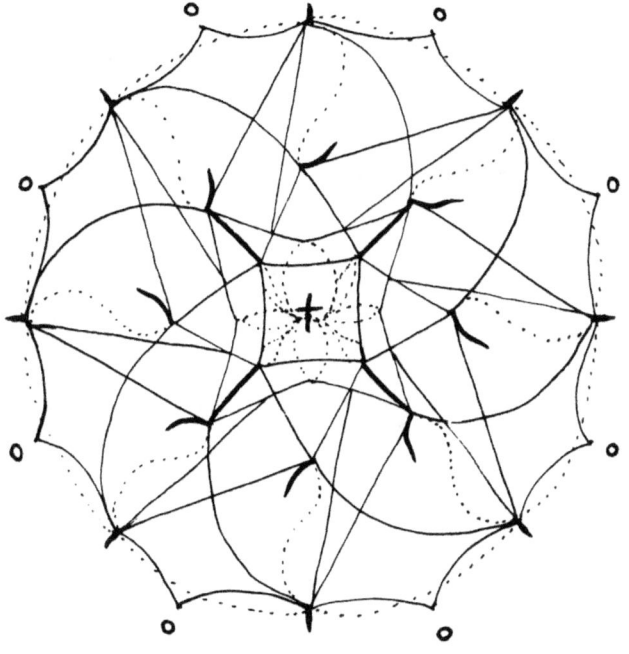

Figure 22

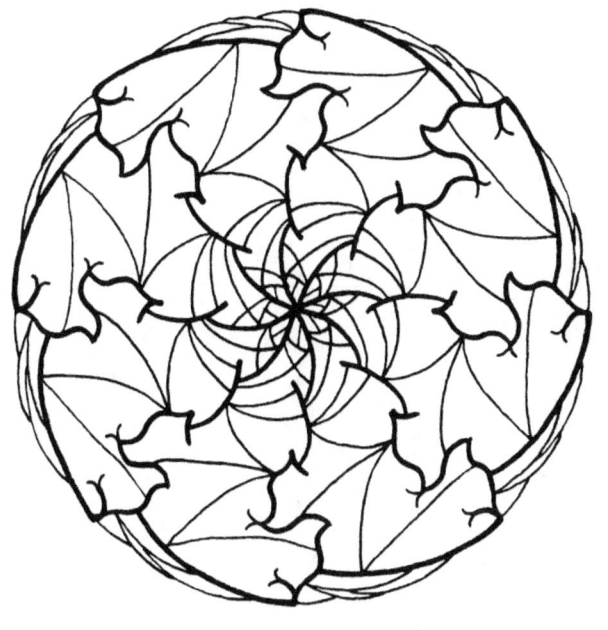

We are invited to participate in the rebuilding
of the world.

Aaron White

Figure 23

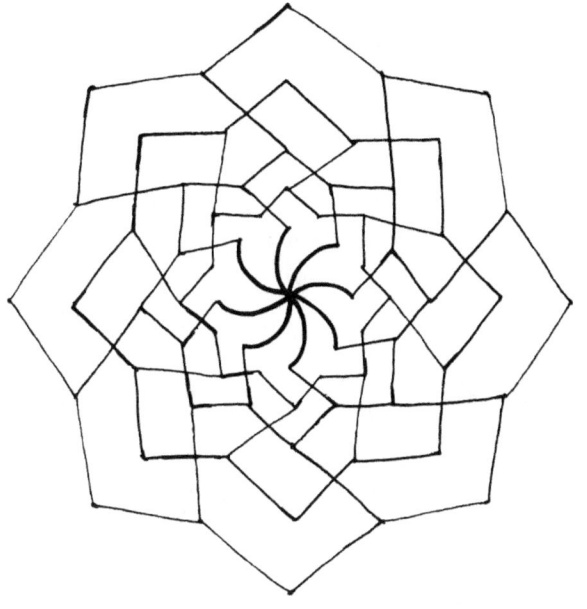

Figure 24

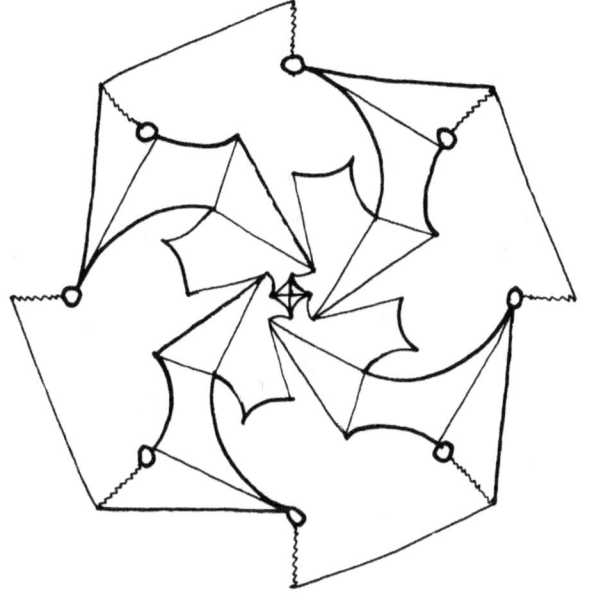

Figure 25

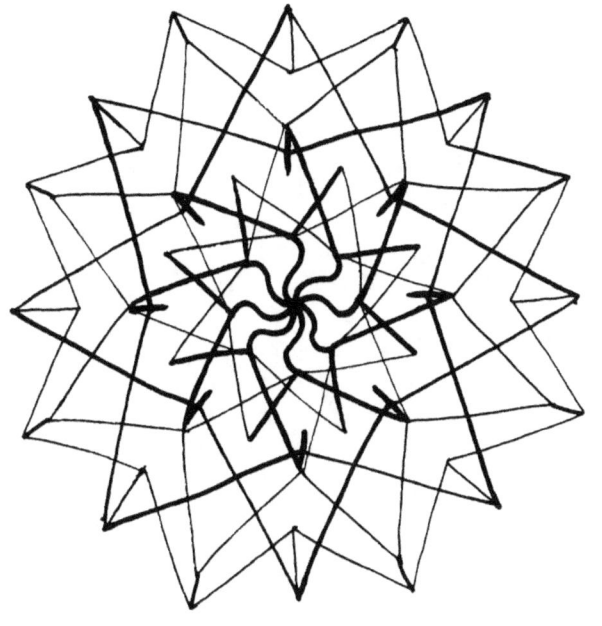

Figure 26

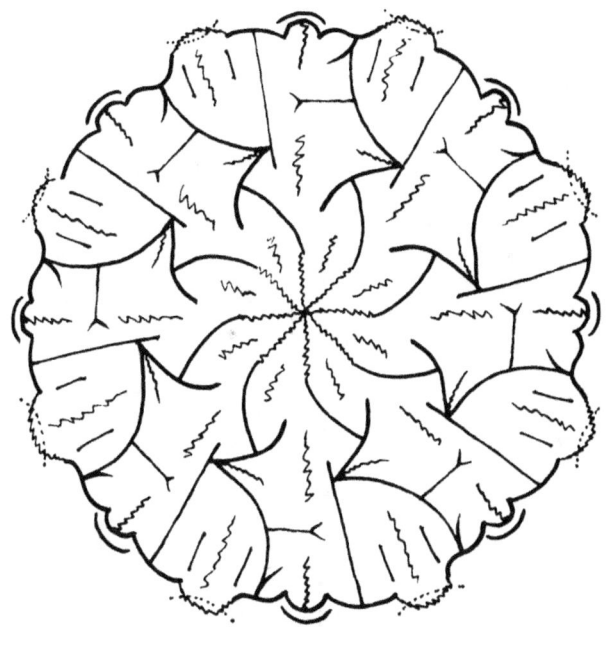

At the threshold, pause — reflect.
Lest we return to Egypt we must always step
forward.

paraphrased from *Daniel Kanter*

Figure 27

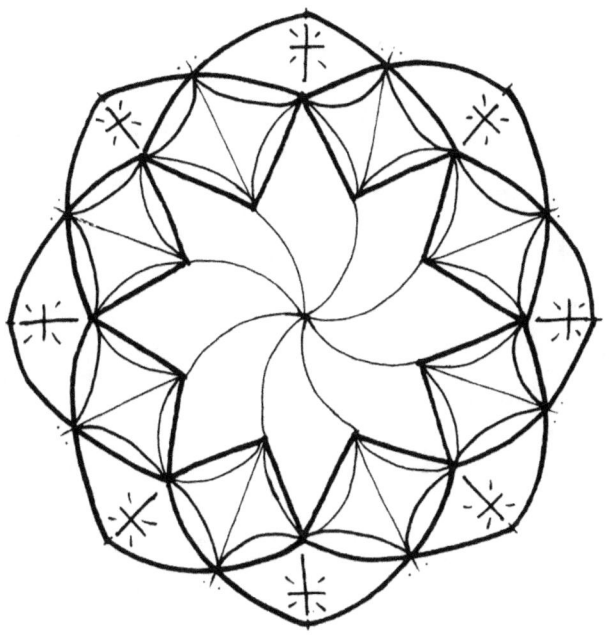

Figure 28

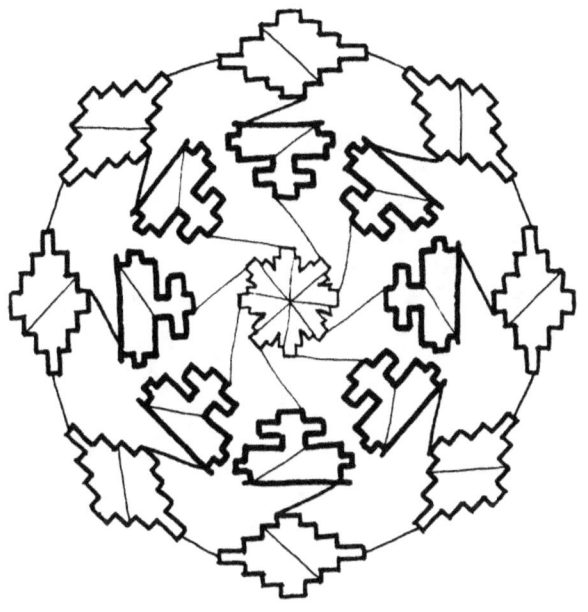

Figure 29

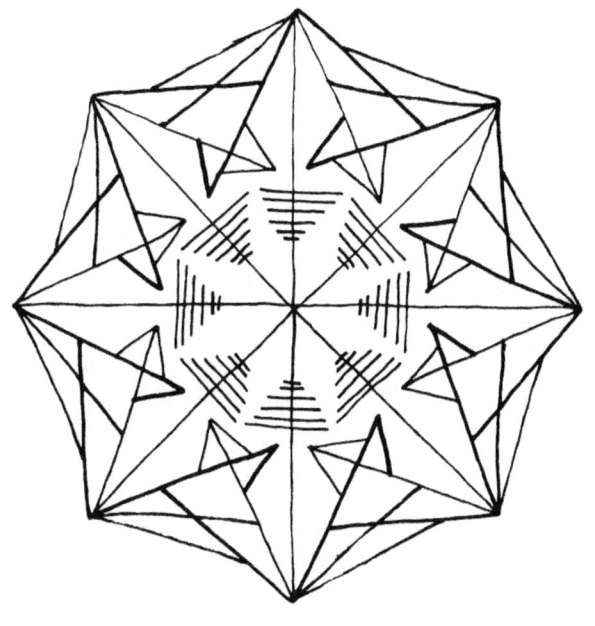

If we prepare for the future, we find out what is important for us today...

Daniel Kanter

Figure 30

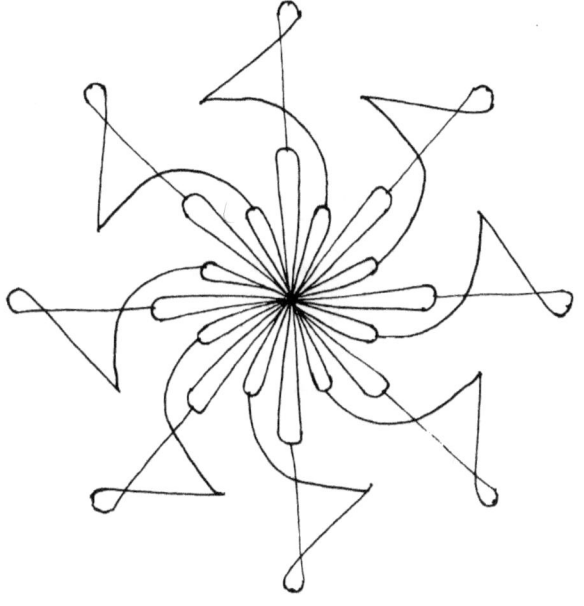

Figure 31

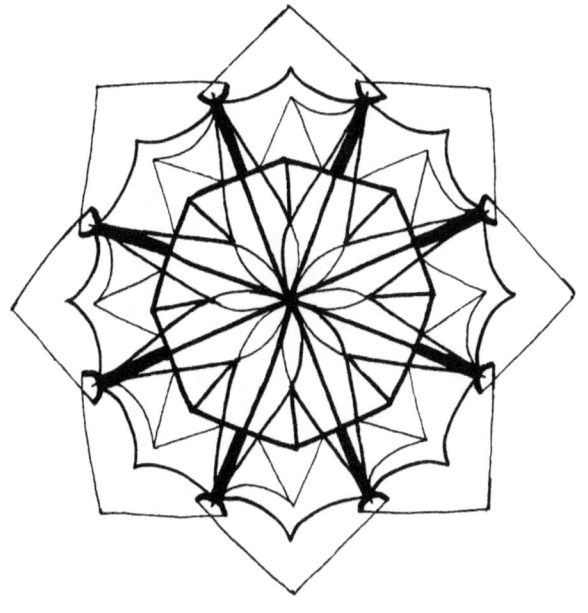

Figure 32

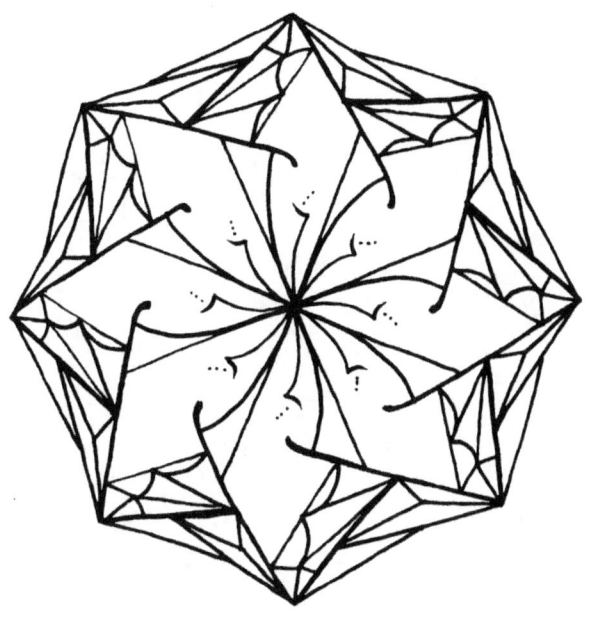

Figure 33

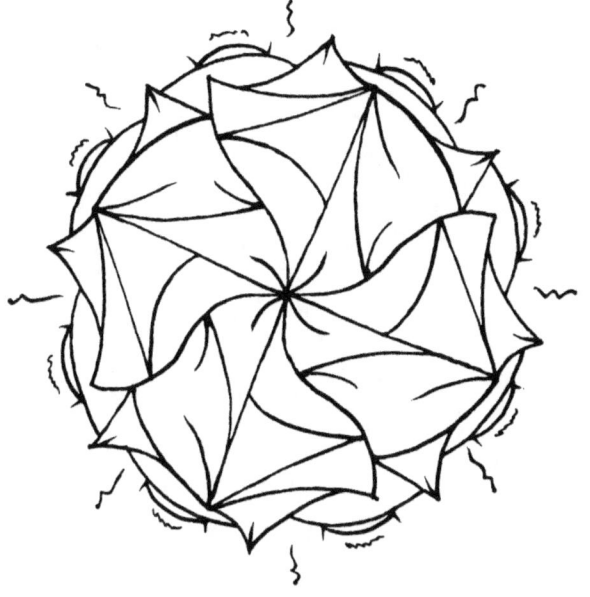

Figure 34

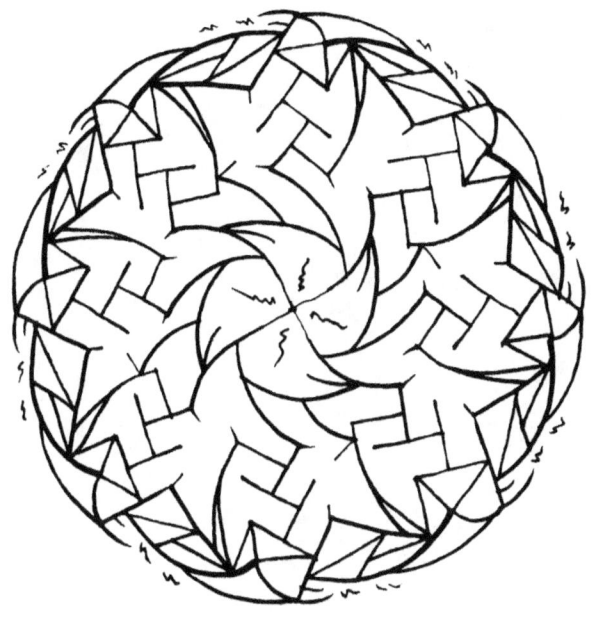

Sometimes the things we think go without
saying need saying again.

Aaron White

Figure 35

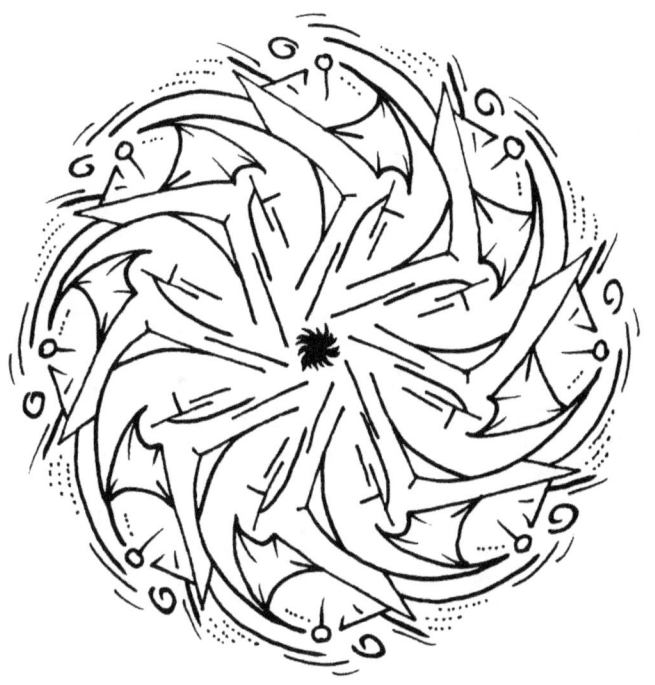

Figure 36

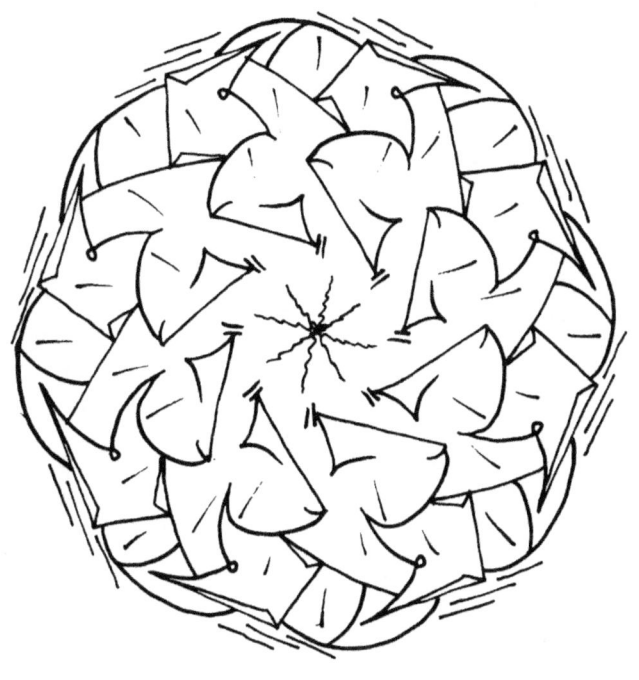

What I most regretted was my silences.
Audre Lorde

Figure 37

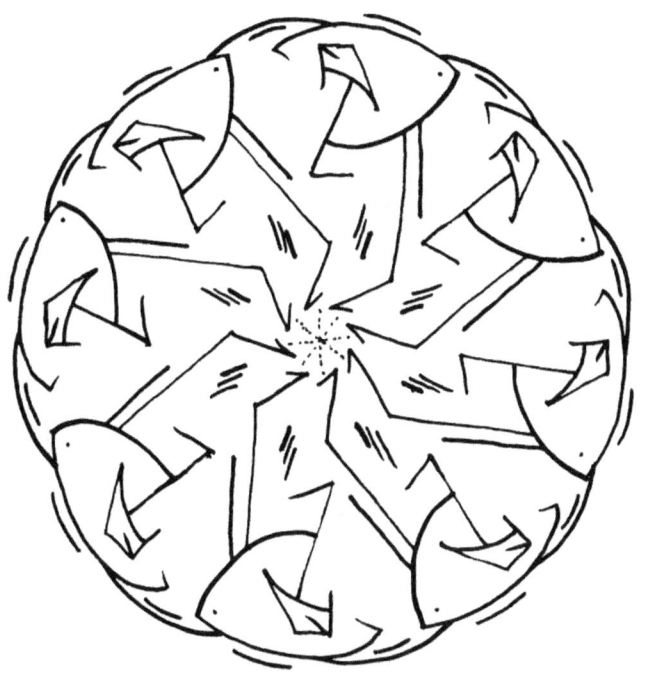

Figure 38

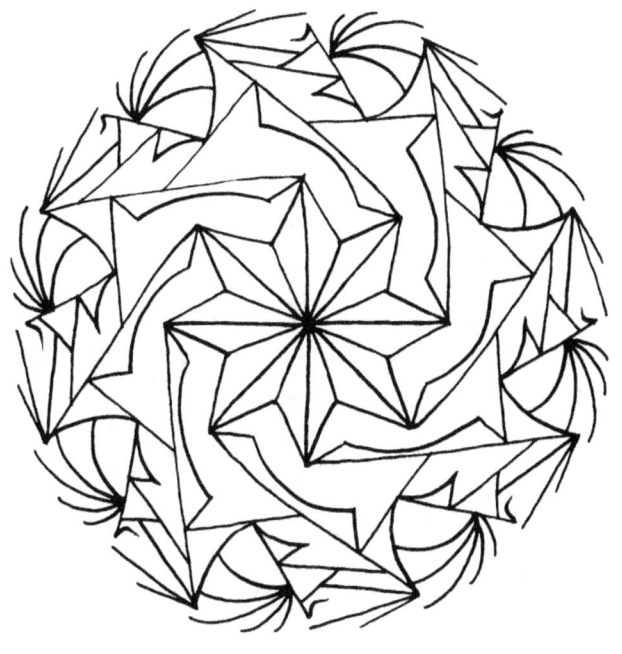

The story is more complex...
Aaron White

Figure 39

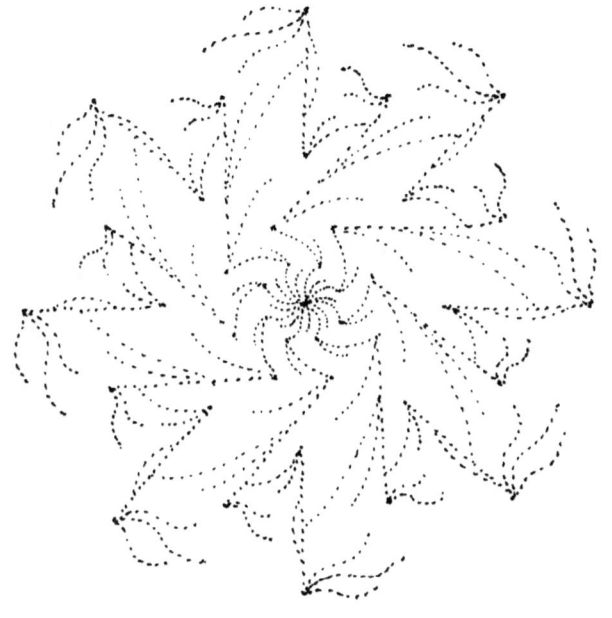

Figure 40

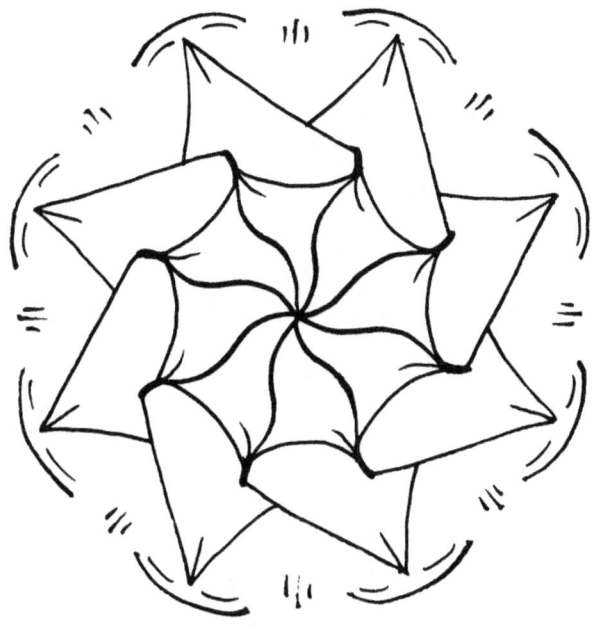

Figure 41

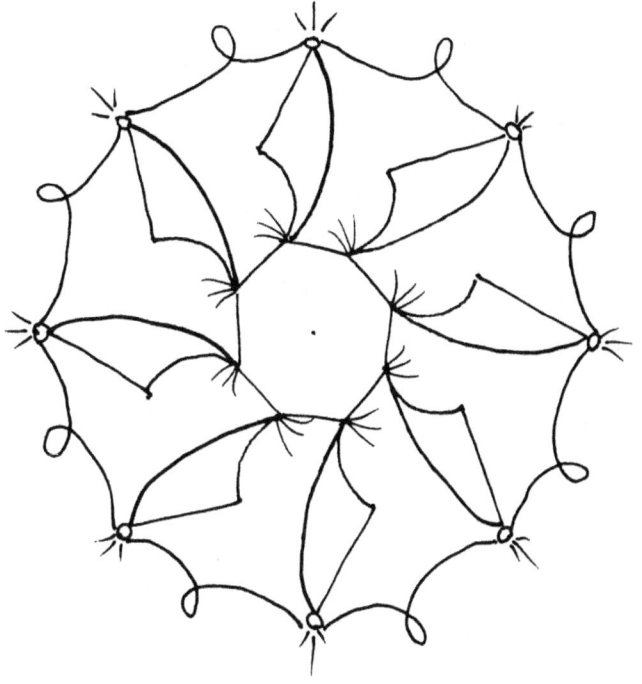

Figure 42

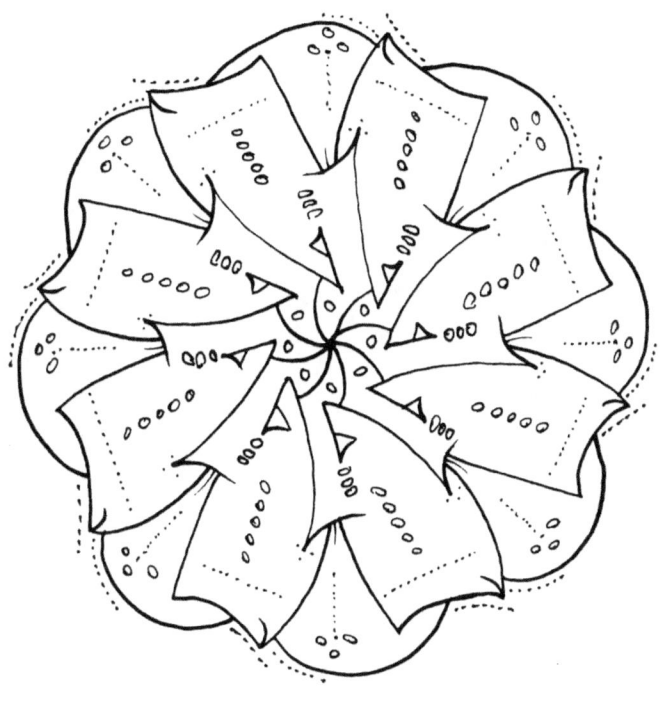

Ask serious questions that are always present
but rarely visited...

Daniel Kanter

Figure 43

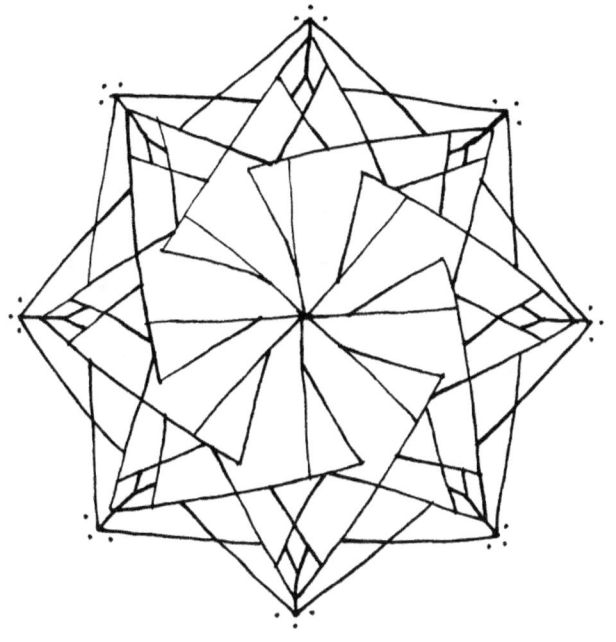

Figure 44

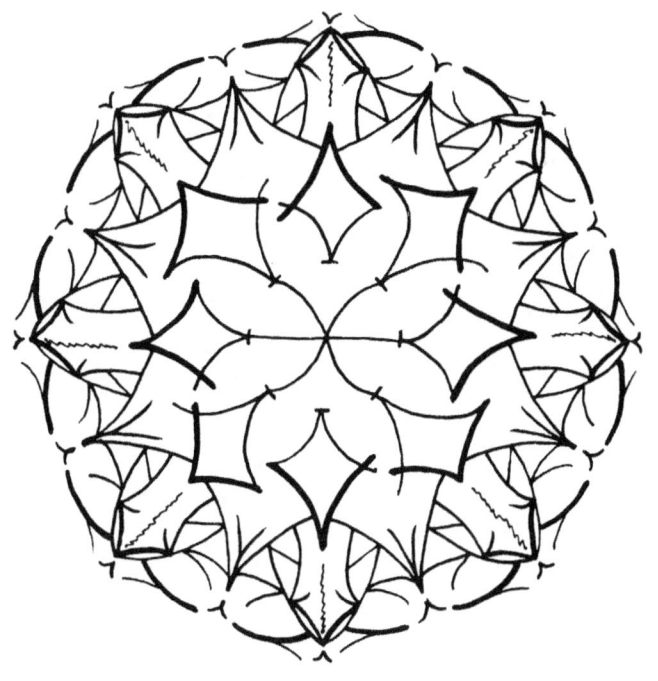

Figure 45

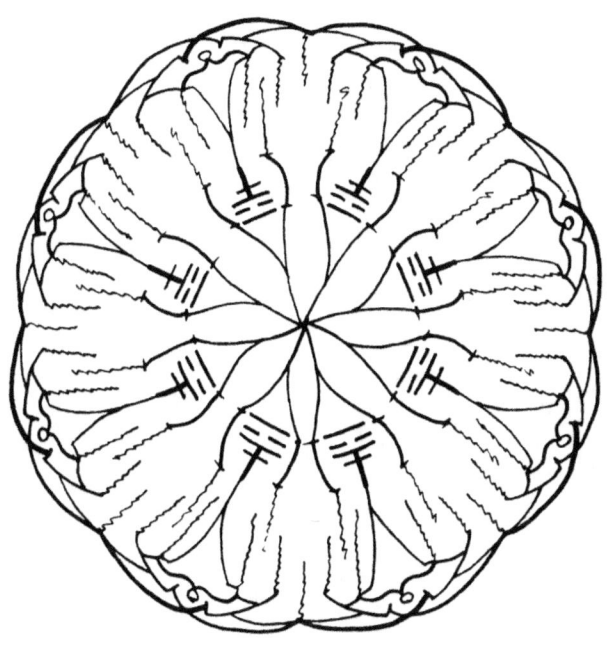

The kingdom of heaven is within our reach...
It is in the decisions we make.

Daniel Kanter

Figure 46

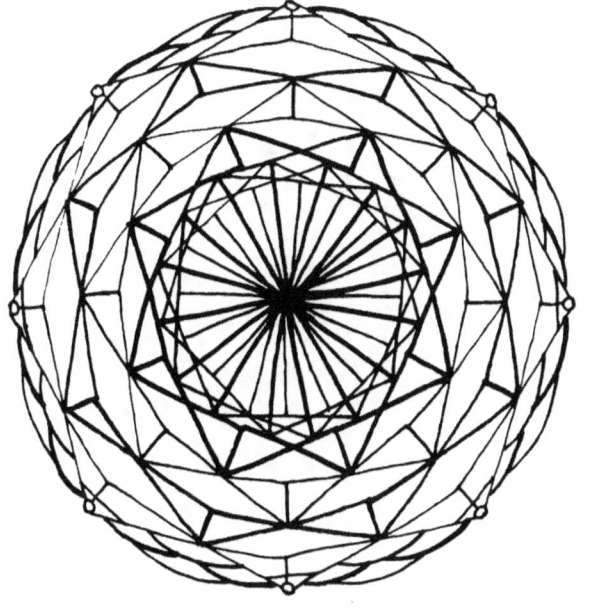

Figure 47

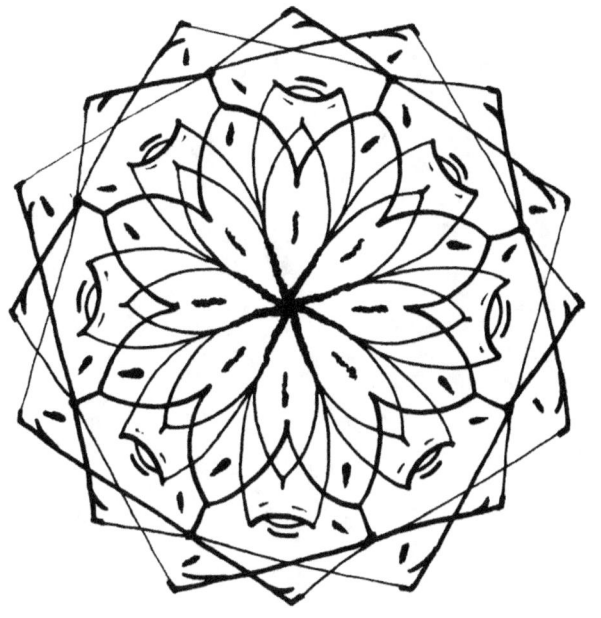

Figure 48

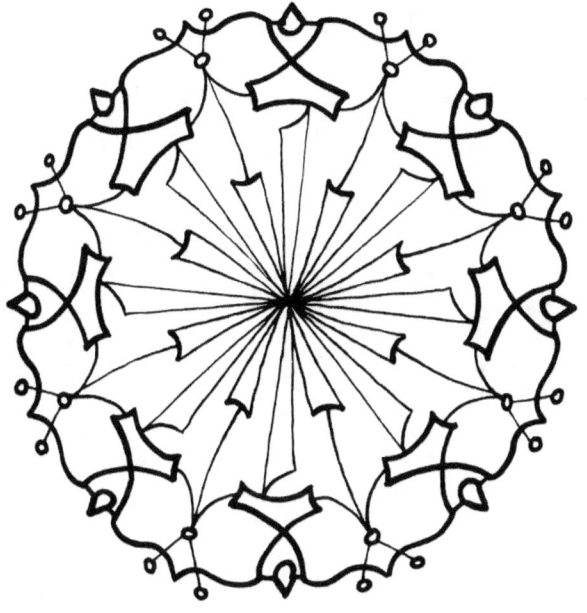

Figure 49

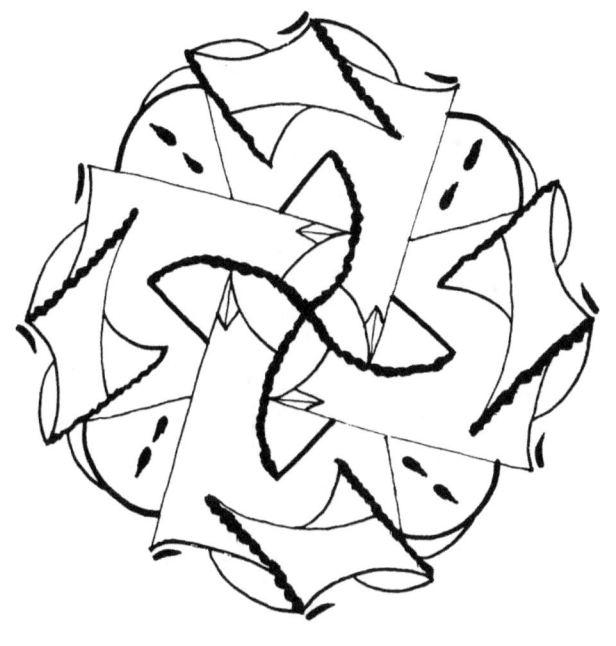

Give up fear... Bring peace.

Daniel Kanter

Figure 50

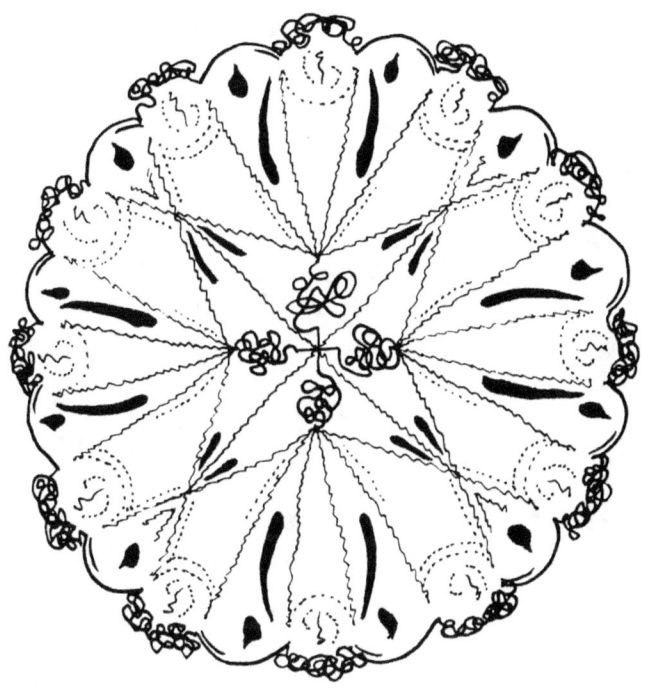

Figure 51

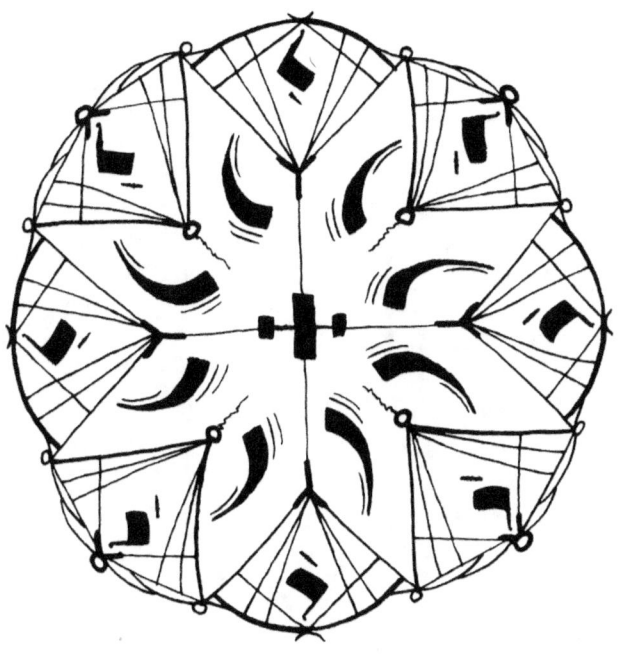

Figure 52

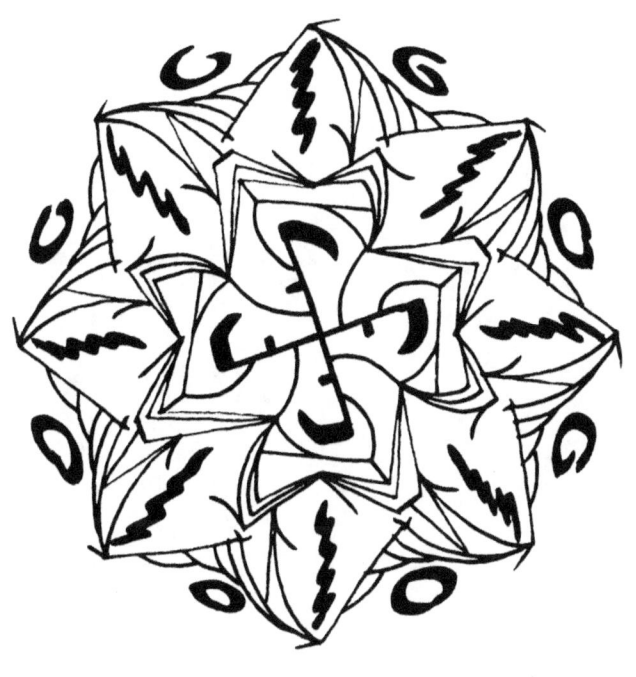

Each of us has the potential to transform the
world.

Aaron White

Figure 53

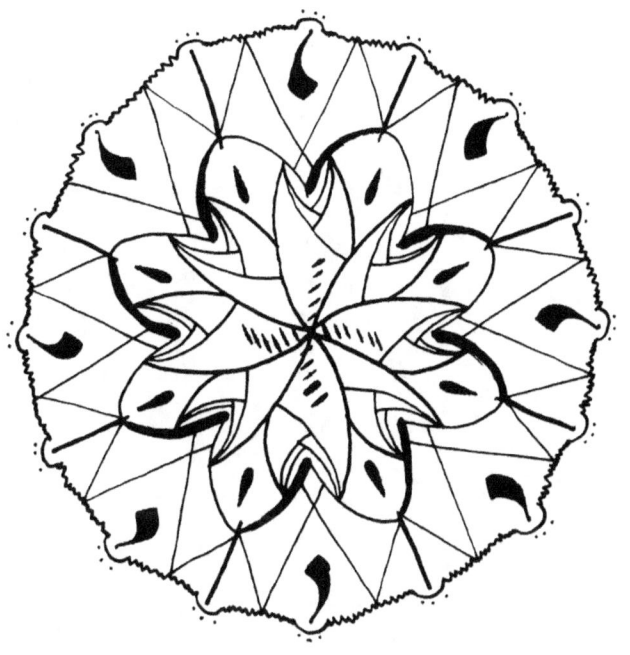

Figure 54

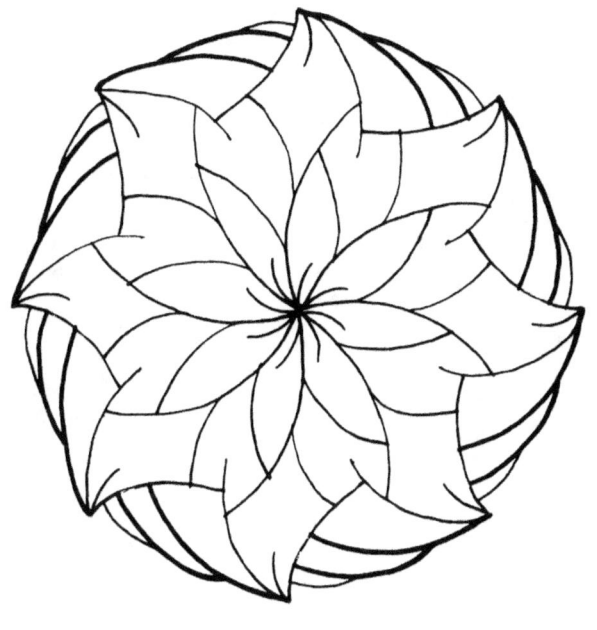

Take your place on The Great Mandala...
You must choose now, win or lose now.

Peter Yarrow

Figure 55

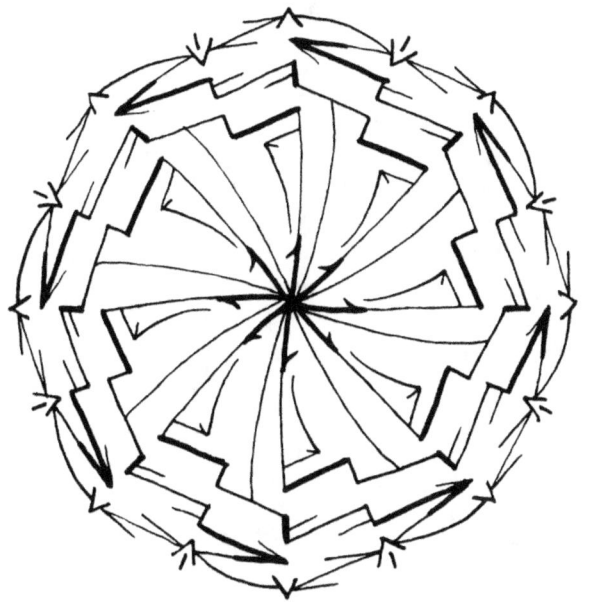

Figure 56

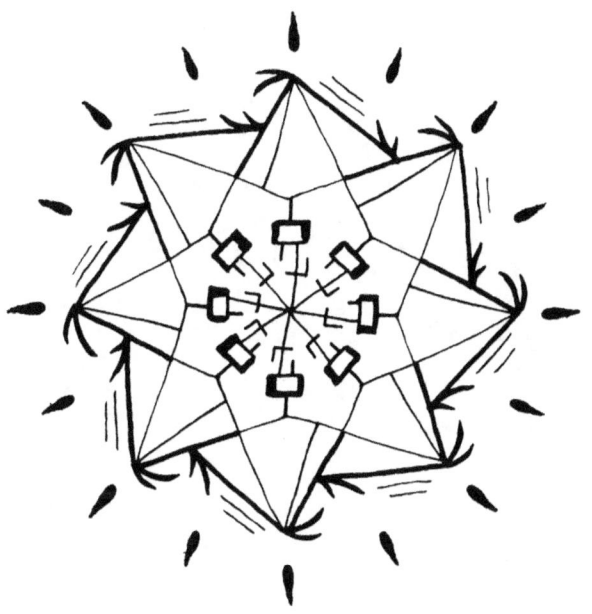

Figure 57

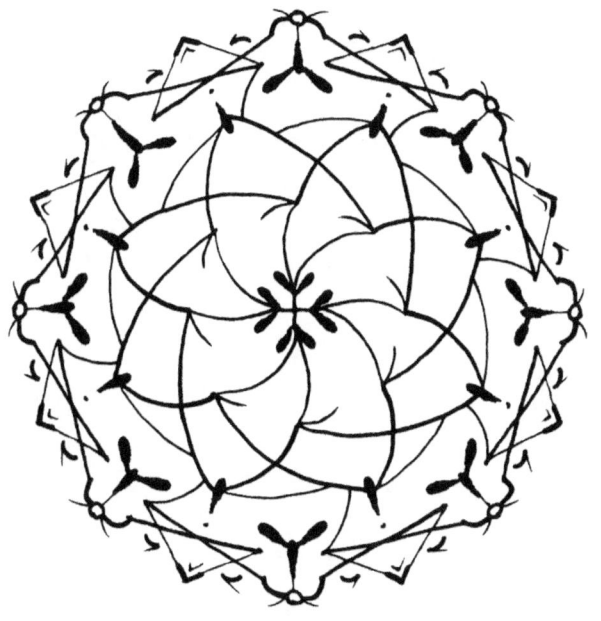

Figure 58

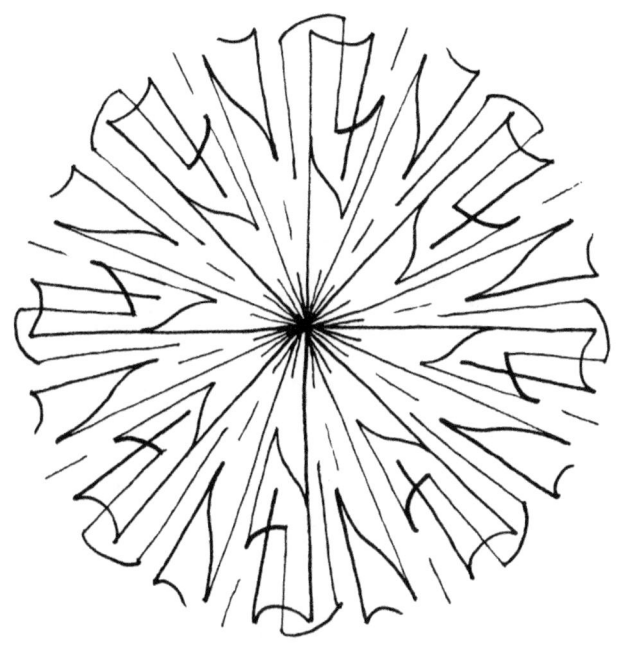

How do we embrace things we will
one day lose?

Aaron White

Figure 59

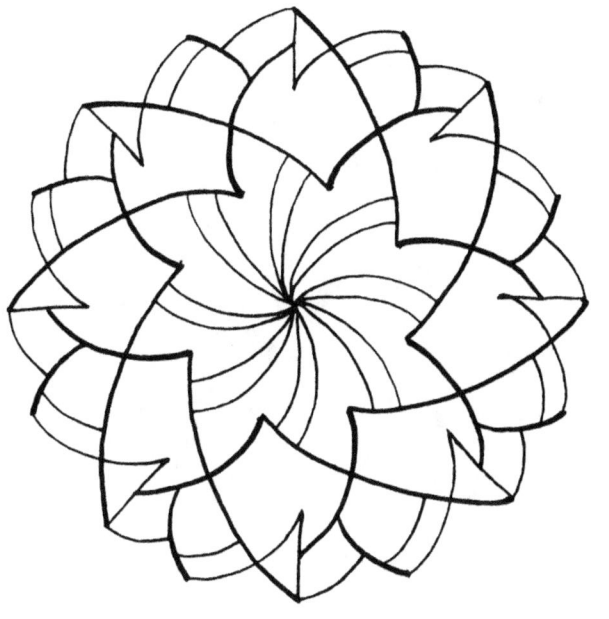

Figure 60

For More

For a video demonstration of Walter drawing a mandala, go to
ninetydays.com/video.

Please visit ninetydays.com and sign up for our email newsletter.